Fascinated by Heaven on Earth

*Seeing Heaven Transform Your Life
and the Lives of Others*

by Mark Crawford

Kingdom Development Group

54 Ridge Road
Legana. 7277
Tasmania
Australia

ISBN -10: 1481999435
ISBN -13: 978-1481999434

Proceeds from the profits of this book will go to Kingdom Development Group (KDG) to enable economic change among people in developing countries.

www.kingdomdevelop.com

Cover by Engram Design
www.engramdesign.com.au

I dedicate this book to my wife, Annette, who has always believed in me and my destiny, even more than I ever believed it.

To Alison and Josh, my two children, who have never ceased to make me proud.

To my mum and dad, who gave me so much and helped me become who I am today.

Thanks for the encouragement and love!

Acknowledgements

Writing a book is both an exciting thing and a lot of hard work. It is due to the help and encouragement of others that you have this book in your hands. I would like to thank the following people in particular.

Annette, my wife and my greatest fan, who has kept encouraging me and finding ways of inspiring me to continue to write. Thanks for your editing and suggestions that have made a world of difference to the final product.

Peter Christensen, for releasing the word in 2001 that declared I was a writer; thanks for being obedient.

Wayne and Pat, for your challenge and encouragement to write and for the editing work; you helped turn something good into something great.

Catherine, for your work on editing; thank you so much for the time and effort you put in.

Josh, my son, what a brilliant design you came up with for the cover, and so quickly; thanks so much.

Alison, my daughter, for your contribution, insightful suggestions, and critique, thank you.

Endorsements

The kingdom of Heaven has been a major theme of my life and reading Mark Crawford's excellent work stirs a fresh desire within to once again be Fascinated by Heaven on Earth. He writes in a simple uncomplicated style that demonstrates he is authentic about his fascination with heaven on earth, and that his hearts desire to help every seeking Christian enter into a new level of relationship with our Heavenly Father. This is a must read for anyone who wants to enter into the quality of life that is available to every genuine Christ follower.

Phillip Mutzelburg
President
A2A (Acts 2 Church Alliance)
www.a2a.org.au

With his strong prophetic gifting, his deep under-standing of the scriptures, and his consistent commitment to seek out the new things of God, Mark Crawford is a voice that needs to be heard by Christians today. He encourages us with deep truths but simple language to become everything the Lord has made and called us to be.

This book is refreshing and revitalising for all those who struggle with the constraints of legalistic church practices, and the resounding truths contained herein will transform your Kingdom ministry – as a pastor, a business leader, a political leader - indeed in all walks of life.

John Dingemanse FAIB FAICD
Designer, Business and Social Entrepreneur
Founder and CEO – CBM Sustainability Group
www.cbmgroup.com.au

If you change the way you look at things, the things you look at change.

–Wayne Dyer

Contents

Acknowledgements. 5

Endorsements 7

Foreword 13

Introduction 17

1. The Day That Everything Changed . . . 19

2. Uniquely Made 27

3. A Son Is Always the Answer 49

4. Holy Spirit 63

5. Earnest Expectation 83

6. Transformation 97

7. Handling the Tough Days. 107

8. The Keys. 125

9. Andrew's Experience: Heaven
   Comes to Earth. 135

Fascinated By Heaven On Earth 143

Foreword

When I first read the title of Mark's new book, I quickly found myself humming the melody to the 1904 waltz "Fascination." I could hear the voice of the great singer Nat King Cole crooning the words of that old love song, "It was fascination, I know. And it might have ended at the start. Just a passing glance, just a brief romance, and I might have gone on my way empty hearted."

The last phrase of what I remembered of the song fascinated me, so I looked up the rest of the lyrics. I pleasantly discovered that the song continues on to reveal that a touch and a kiss leave the lover anything but empty hearted. "It was fascination, I know, seeing you alone with the moonlight above. Then I touch your hand,

and next moment I kiss you. Fascination turned to love."

You may be wondering what the lyrics to Fermo Marchetti's beautiful melody, written over a century ago, have in common with this book.

One thing: love.

God could have left us empty hearted, only allowing us to see him from afar, but he was fascinated with us, came down to be with us, touched us, and kissed us. It is absolutely true that we are gloriously held captive in a divine love triangle.

As my friend Joel Butz explains, God the Father is the lover, Jesus is the beloved, the Holy Spirit is the kiss between them, and we are caught in the embrace...that is heaven on earth! How could you not be fascinated by the majesty, intimacy, and pure joy of all that love?

I have known Mark Crawford for over ten years and can say with hand on heart that what you will read in this book is authentic to how Mark goes about life. He is truly, completely fascinated with the kingdom of God and has given his life to advance it. Heaven on Earth, the increase of God's kingdom in our world, is the meditation of his heart and is the longing that motivates and energizes his vision.

In Fascinated by Heaven on Earth, you will have the opportunity to step through windows of revelation that will open you to a lifestyle of dispensing heavenly grace into your world, no matter what your calling or occupation. Mark gives a unique perspective that will cause you to think differently, and if you will allow, will change the way you live. If the longing of your heart is to be an agent of heaven on Earth, this book is a must read.

David Crone
Senior Leader at The Mission, Vacaville, California
Author of Decisions That Define Us, The Power of Your Life Message, and Declarations That Empower Us.
www.davecrone.com

Introduction

On August 24, 2001, I received a powerful, lengthy, and significant word from a prophet named Peter Christensen in Australia.

This word contained declarations that I was called to be a writer, among other things, some of which have already happened.

I now realize that that prophetic word was also the start of my journey toward understanding the reality of Heaven on Earth.

Every day since that time, my fascination with Heaven coming to Earth has only increased.

There is no end to God or Heaven, and it is a lot of fun finding new things to discover and living on Earth.

My friend David Crone's foreword wonderfully describes the type of fascination we are meant to have with Heaven and its impact on Earth.

My prayer is that this book will somehow touch you so much that you will want to change, embrace the truths contained within, and never be the same.

Chapter 1

The Day That Everything Changed

The air is full of expectancy, and the day seems so wonderfully different from any other day. The sun is shining brightly, and it's getting hot. Streams of sunlight are hitting the waters of the Jordan River, sending out shafts of light and creating a kaleidoscope of color.

There are sounds of birds and crickets blending together yet still sounding distinctively different. Then there is the sound of voices carrying across the desolate land, many voices, but one voice easily heard above the rest. It's a strong, powerful voice that captivates the listener, permeating your thoughts and drawing you closer to the one speaking. It's almost irresistible, compelling, but at the same time daunting.

What is he saying? What is it that he is declaring? It's time to repent, think differently, change your mind, regret your sins, and change your conduct, for the kingdom of Heaven is nearby. These are new words; they have not heard this talk before.

There are so many people all around the place who are wanting to be baptized. The religious men are there and wanting to be baptized too. What is this man called John saying? He seems to be telling them that they are like a brood of vipers and not making friends with them at all.

A solitary figure approaches from the distance, a man in his early thirties. There is nothing about him that stands out, but you know he is special—for some reason, you can't define why. If only you could determine why he is so special. Maybe it's the way he walks, the way he looks into your eyes, and the love that flows into you as he talks; maybe it's the way he holds his head confidently and he holds himself in such a royal manner. Maybe it's the atmosphere of peace all around him.

John, the one doing the talking, really stands out. His clothes are so different from everyone else's: he wears camel's hair clothes with a wide leather belt. His breath has this strange, sweet, yet savory smell about it.

Quietly, this solitary person, Jesus, approaches John, and it does not take long for John to recognize him—firstly, as his cousin, and then as someone far more significant, as the Messiah.

Jesus wants John to baptize him, and immediately John protests quite strenuously. "Me, baptize you? You're the one that ought to be baptizing me!" After some discussion John relents and agrees to baptize Jesus.

The crowd knows something significant is happening though it looks just like all the rest of the baptisms. Still, it seems different, regal; there is a feeling that history is being created right now.

At last John baptizes Jesus, and as he comes up out of the water, things become even brighter. It is as though the heavens have opened up and the atmosphere has changed suddenly. It is so tangible that you can feel the change. It is heaviness, but not a bad heaviness; it is the "lifting you up" type of atmosphere that causes you to feel suddenly good about life and everything else.

Then a dove flies down and comes to sit upon Jesus. I am telling you, it is no ordinary dove. It is just, well, special—hard to describe, but everyone knew it was important.

Suddenly a voice, sounding like thunder, comes from the heavens. It's a commanding voice but also a familiar, loving voice. It's God speaking, and he says, "This is my Son, my beloved Son, in whom I am well pleased."

Wow! This is the first occasion in all of history that God has introduced himself as a father. A new era has begun; we have just been ushered into a new relationship with God. This is the time of knowing and experiencing him as our Father in Heaven.

Until this moment in time, the people on Earth knew about God, but they had only known him from a distance.

It was just as Bette Midler sang in her 1990 hit song, "From a Distance":

We are instruments
Marching in a common band
Playing songs of hope
Playing songs of peace
They are the songs of every man
God is watching us
God is watching us
God is watching us
From a distance.

We had been so concerned up to this time that we might use God's name in vain that we used all sorts of words to describe him, and yet he still remained a far-off God.

This was never his plan, and he wanted to be known and experienced as our Father. He wanted us to be fascinated with him and his ways, just as much as he was fascinated with us and our future.

So it is time once again to regain the fascination with Heaven and its place on Earth. There is a proverb that says,

> *A satisfied soul loathes the honeycomb,*
> *But to a hungry soul every bitter thing is sweet.* **Proverbs 27:7**

This describes someone who is so satisfied with things, with life that even the delicacy of something special like honeycomb has no appeal any more. However, the hungry person finds every single thing to be delightful and desirable. It seems that the position you adopt determines what you get in your future.

If you stop eating food, you get hungry. I have fasted on many occasions, and I don't know why they call it fasting when it goes so slow. I think it

23

should be renamed slowing! Anyway, not eating food makes you hungry. However, in the realm of the spirit, eating makes you hungry for more. Partaking of the things of Heaven makes room for more.

Satisfied people are no longer fascinated with the things of Heaven. In fact, these things have become ho-hum to them. Remember, I did not say thankful people, I said satisfied people. It is time once again to become fascinated with Heaven coming to Earth, to see Heaven influential on Earth. Time to partake of the more!

I invite you to discover afresh what it is to be fascinated with Heaven on Earth.

I am fascinated with the truth that God is my Father in Heaven.

Today:

To help appropriate a new mindset, consider who you describe God as. Can you start privately to call him Father, Papa, or even Daddy? Declare also today that "my Father in Heaven is near and dear to me."

In this chapter we discovered:

1. The amazing impact that the baptism of Jesus had upon our lives.

2. God as our Father and how he longs for us to know him intimately yet majestically.

3. That our Father in Heaven has already declared aloud that we are children of his, beloved children, and that he is well pleased with us.

4. That it is important to be a thankful person but not satisfied, understanding that the more we partake of the spiritual, the hungrier we are for more.

Chapter 2

Uniquely Made

Isn't it amazing that we are all made in God's image, and yet there is so much diversity among his people?
–Desmond Tutu

If there is one message, one theme, that has fascinated me for a long time and that the Father has had me focus on, one that has changed me the most, it is the message of who I am.

I have preached this so many times, so many different ways, to so many different groups of people in different nations that at times I have asked the Father, "Can't I preach something else?" He just seems to smile at me and let me have my moment before I preach what he asks me. I am convinced that you can never hear enough about who we are in Christ.

The more you understand about who God is, the more you will understand who you are, and the more you understand who you are, the more you understand who God is. This goes on and on into eternity for this cycle has no end, like an upward spiral.

The Father challenges our thinking constantly, causing us to come into a place where we need to change.

For if we always do what we have always done, we will always get what we have always got.

The kingdom of Heaven is so much about exchange; exchanging what you have for what he has, what exists in Heaven. When that happens, you are bringing Heaven to Earth; you are causing his will to be done on Earth as it is in Heaven.

Unless you are willing to give him what you have, you won't get what he has. It's like the trapeze artist moving from one swing to another. As long as he keeps hanging onto the first swing, he is not going to take the second swing. Of course, there is the frightful moment of being in between swings, neither hanging onto the first swing nor the second one, in no man's land!

Unless you let go of the swing, you will not take the next swing and complete the maneuver.

I heard it said recently that, "In the beginning God made the Heavens and the Earth; everything else was made in China!"

> *Then God said, "Let Us make man in Our image, according to Our likeness; let them have dominion over the fish of the sea, over the birds of the air, and over the cattle, over all the earth and over every creeping thing that creeps on the earth." So God created man in His own image; in the image of God He created him; male and female He created them. Then God blessed them, and God said to them, "Be fruitful and multiply; fill the earth and subdue it; have dominion over the fish of the sea, over the birds of the air, and over every living thing that moves on the earth."*
> **Genesis 1:26–28**

Man was created in the image of God, not God but like him.

It is significant that God made mankind in his image, and there are many aspects of that nature that we ought to explore.

Let me explore just a few with you.

The incredible mystery exists that God is three in one: the Father, the Son, and the Holy Spirit. They are so unified that you cannot separate them, but they are three distinct beings. This is such a mystery to us that we find it impossible to comprehend completely. We will have all of eternity to discover more about it.

Tripartite Beings

As we are made in the image of the Trinity, we are made as tripartite beings. In the image of God—the Father, the Son, and the Holy Spirit. We have three parts to us—body, soul, and spirit. You can describe them and experience them, but you cannot separate the parts.

Each of those parts requires fuel; specific fuel for each tank. Body fuel, such as eating, sleeping, and exercise, will fill the body tank. No other fuel will work. The soul has three parts as well: the thinking (mind), feeling (emotions), and choosing (will) parts.

Soul fuel is for the soul tank—no other fuel will work. Soul fuel differs for every person but can be things such as socializing, reading a good book, watching a movie, a romantic dinner or event, eating, sports, mountain climbing, or retail therapy.

Spirit fuel is designed specifically for the spirit tank: praying, fellowship, worship, speaking in tongues, and fasting.

It is important to know the fuel that fills your different tanks and to be deliberate about keeping your fuel tanks at least half full. It is my observation that people who let their fuel tanks get too low have a difficult time filling them up.

The soul is designed to be a bridge between the body and the spirit to connect the physical with the spiritual. It is a good servant but a poor master. We are meant to be led by the spirit.

Choice is probably the greatest gift we have. We have been given the ability to choose. Don't believe the lie that we don't have choices. In fact, once you come to Christ, there is an even greater ability to choose.

And if it seems evil to you to serve the Lord, choose for yourselves this day whom you will serve, whether the gods which your fathers served that were on the other side of the river, or the gods of the Amorites, in whose land you dwell. But as for me and my house, we will serve the Lord."
Joshua 24:15

Community

God has always existed in community and relationship. He is community and he lives from a position of community. All governance positions are meant to operate out of a relational paradigm.

Some people say that God needed to have human beings on Earth in order to love. There is no need in God or Heaven, so that is a complete misunderstanding! It would be better stated that God wanted human beings to commune with.

You must interpret everything that God does through the paradigm of community. If you don't, you will not understand what he means. There is much misunderstanding about God's ways because so often they are not interpreted through his nature.

So we are made for community—relationships.

All of scripture is about protecting and growing relationships. Relational values and principles are contained in the scriptures from Genesis to Revelation.

The Father always wants to demonstrate his nature, and relationship and community are part of that nature. His very core being is established in community.

The Father, the Son, and the Holy Spirit are in a perfect relationship with each other.

Jesus told us,

> *"You shall love the Lord your God with all your heart, with all your soul, and with all your mind."*
> *This is the first and great commandment. And the second is like it: "You shall love your neighbor as yourself." On these two commandments hang all the Law and the Prophets.*
> **Matthew 22:36–40**

This passage describes the two critical relationships of anyone's life: relationship with God and relationship with others.

Community is where we learn to function in relationship with others. We are not made to do life on our own, no matter what we feel, what personality type we are, or whether we are extroverted or introverted.

So many believers fail to understand that, instead of running away from difficult relational issues, we are meant to stay and put them right. We bless the Father when we do that and place ourselves in a place to be blessed.

> *Therefore if you bring your gift to the altar, and there remember that your brother has something against you, leave your gift there before the altar, and go your way. First be reconciled to your brother, and then come and offer your gift.*
> **Matthew 5:23–24**

The Father will often tell someone else something for you that he could have told you directly;

he always wants to reinforce community. It's who he is—community.

Health

We are made for health—that's why our bodies struggle with sickness. The Father does not just "do" healing; he is health. There is no sickness in Heaven. One touch from Heaven heals! Our bodies are designed to heal themselves. They are not made for sickness. So, it makes an amazing difference if you look at any sickness that comes to you from a position of health. You direct your body to reject sickness because you're not designed to have it. You command sickness to leave because you are made for health.

Generosity

Our Father in Heaven is incredibly generous.

> *For God so loved the world that He gave His only begotten Son, that whoever believes in Him should not perish but have everlasting life.* **John 3:16**

So we are designed and made to be generous, and anything less than that will cause you to feel inferior.

> *The world of the generous gets larger and larger; the world of the stingy gets smaller and smaller.*
> **Proverbs 11:24 MSG**

We are always meant to be expanding; that is, looking for larger and larger influence in the world. Transformation is the goal. Generosity is the key to our enlargement.

We are meant to be great givers and excellent receivers. Free to give beyond our restrictions and receive beyond what feels comfortable. We are meant to be rivers flowing, not dams holding water.

Most people begin strong in one or the other; they are either naturally great givers or naturally great receivers. Therefore the givers have to learn how to receive and the receivers have to learn how to give. The Father wants us to return to who we were made to be—outrageously generous people who know how to receive wonderfully.

Faith, Hope, and Love

We are made for faith. We are made to operate in the faith realm—to believe, to hope, to love. We are not made for doubt, unbelief, or fear. It's why we suffer so much when we are caught in hopelessness.

Heaven's default position is YES—his promises are yes and amen.

When we operate in each of these areas, we step into who we were meant to be. But something happened that complicated things, something that changed all that was meant to have been.

Lucifer was an archangel in Heaven, in charge of worship.

> *How you are fallen from Heaven,*
> *O Lucifer, son of the morning! How*
> *you are cut down to the ground,*
> *You who weakened the nations!*
> *For you have said in your heart:*
> *"I will ascend into Heaven, I will*
> *exalt my throne above the stars of*
> *God; I will also sit on the mount of*
> *the congregation On the farthest*
> *sides of the north; I will ascend*
> *above the heights of the clouds,*

*I will be like the Most High." Yet you
shall be brought down to Sheol,
To the lowest depths of the Pit.
Those who see you will gaze at
you, And consider you, saying: "Is
this the man who made the earth
tremble, who shook Kingdoms?"*
Isaiah 14:12–16

Everything that Lucifer had wanted and desired to the point of rebellion got him evicted from Heaven. He became Satan, and now we have been given all he wanted and more! That's why he so hates us so much. He is angry with the fact that we were so readily given what he wanted.

He said, "I will ascend into Heaven," but together we have been seated in heavenly places.

He said, "I will be like the most high," but we have been created in his image.

He wanted authority, but we have become children of God. In our relationship with him, we have authority, position, and influence—all that Lucifer wanted.

Everything that Lucifer desired in his heart, the Father gave to us, and he placed desires in our heart for these things.

*He has made everything beautiful
in its time. Also He has put eternity in their hearts, except that
no one can find out the work that
God does from beginning to end.*
Ecclesiastes 3:11

Through the cross Jesus, as the last Adam, reclaimed all that we were to have inherited with the first Adam and more. We now have become the carriers of Heaven.

If we move through Genesis and into the third chapter, we see Satan (Lucifer) approaching Eve in the Garden and talking to her.

*Now the serpent was more cun-
ning than any beast of the field
which the Lord God had made.
And he said to the woman, "Has
God indeed said, 'You shall not eat
of every tree of the garden'?" And
the woman said to the serpent,
"We may eat the fruit of the trees
of the garden; but of the fruit of
the tree which is in the midst of
the garden, God has said, 'You
shall not eat it, nor shall you touch
it, lest you die.' "*

Then the serpent said to the woman, "You will not surely die. For God knows that in the day you eat of it your eyes will be opened, and you will be like God, knowing good and evil." **Genesis 3:1–5**

Recently I was with some Australian Aboriginal church leaders and they told me that the world would not be in the situation it is right now if Adam and Eve had been Australian Aboriginals. I quizzically asked why. "Well," said one of the leaders, "if they had been Australian Aboriginals, they would have thrown away the apple and eaten the snake."

The enemy always questions what God has said to you, today, tomorrow, or last year. His plan is to cause you to question whether you really have heard from God or not. He wants you to doubt your ability to hear, doubt what you heard, and doubt that God has spoken to you.

Satan specializes in producing doubt and unbelief in your mind.

Choosing to believe that God said what he said, with no question in your mind, will protect you from this onslaught.

Satan asks Eve what God has said to them and draws her into his discussion. Then he, the father of lies, tells her that God has lied to her and indicates that God has held back information from them both. He still does this today, trying to convince us that what is truthful is false and that lies are, in fact, truth.

Then, Satan introduced a major lie to the human race. He said, "If you eat the fruit" (that is, if you do something), "then you will become like God" (that is, you become someone special).

However, Adam and Eve were already like God!

The enemy always tries to get you to work for something that's already yours and that has already been paid for.

He wants you to feel like you can never arrive, that you must be always striving, always trying to become someone special. You can become so busy working for something that you don't have time to live and experience what you already have.

Anytime you strive for something that is already yours by grace, you have placed yourself under the law.

The enemy will tell you that if you just try harder, you can become more like God, when you are already like him.

Let us fast forward to the New Testament and to the story that started this book, the baptism of Jesus in the Jordan River.

Then Jesus came from Galilee to John at the Jordan to be baptized by him. And John tried to prevent Him, saying, "I need to be baptized by You, and are You coming to me?"

But Jesus answered and said to him, "Permit it to be so now, for thus it is fitting for us to fulfil all righteousness." Then he allowed Him. When He had been baptized, Jesus came up immediately from the water; and behold, the Heavens were opened to Him, and He saw the Spirit of God descending like a dove and alighting upon Him. And suddenly a voice came from Heaven, saying, "This is My beloved Son, in whom I am well pleased." **Matthew 3:13–17**

The heavens were opened, and this was the answer to Isaiah's plea:

Oh, that You would rend the Heavens! That You would come down! That the mountains might

shake at Your presence.
Isaiah 64:1

Today the heavens have been opened, and there is now no such thing as "closed heavens." I recall Bill Johnson saying that the only closed heavens today are between believers' left and right ears.

> *But of Him you are in Christ Jesus, who became for us wisdom from God—and righteousness and sanctification and redemption.*
> **1 Corinthians 1:30**

We are in Christ. Now we live and move and have our being in him who saved us.

When Jesus was baptized, we were in him then. We were yet to be born, but the Father saw us who were yet to come into life.

The Father always looks from the end of time back to the present days. He was declaring in the present moment at the Jordan River what was yet to happen as if it had happened then, that day.

*God, who gives life to the dead
and calls those things which do
not exist as though they did.*
Romans 4:17

He said of you on that day, "This is my beloved son or daughter in whom I am well pleased."

And nothing has changed.

When the Father made that declaration, Jesus had not yet started his ministry. He had not yet walked on water, raised the dead, healed the sick, or fed five thousand hungry men. He had not been to the cross or developed the disciples. He had done nothing noteworthy that we know of. And yet the Father declared that he was well pleased.

What we need to understand is that the love that God talks about is not based on how we perform, or what we do or don't do.

There is nothing that can make the Father love you any more or any less than he loves you right now. In fact, he loved you as he loves you now before you knew him. His love is expressed for all mankind, whether they are in the family or not.

His blessings, favor, and rewards are different; they come from how you behave or how you live.

> *But God, who is rich in mercy, because of His great love with which He loved us, even when we were dead in trespasses, made us alive together with Christ (by grace you have been saved), and raised us up together, and made us sit together in the Heavenly places in Christ Jesus, that in the ages to come He might show the exceeding riches of His grace in His kindness toward us in Christ Jesus.* **Ephesians 2:4–7**

I am fascinated that we are made in his image!

Today:

In order to grow in your experience of who you are, I suggest that you regularly declare one of the attributes of God that you want to grow in. That is, say aloud who you are. Keep doing this until you believe it.

For example, declare, "I am a generous person who knows how to receive." You can find many ways to say it to yourself. After all, you most likely talked yourself into the other way of thinking. Also look for ways to be generous.

You can take any of the descriptions above, like health, faith, hope, and love.

In this chapter we discovered:

1. That the kingdom of Heaven is so much about exchanging what you have for what Heaven has.

2. We are made in the image of God and therefore made according to his nature.

3. We are made as tripartite beings with a body, a soul, and a spirit, and each part requires fuel specific for that part.

4. We are made for community and relationships.

5. We are made for health and not for sickness.

6. We are made to be generous and need to be great givers and excellent receivers.

7. We are made for faith, hope, and love.

8. The Father's love for us is not based on our performance. He can't love us any more or any less that he does right now!

Chapter 3

A Son Is Always the Answer

*Royalty is my identity. Servanthood
is my assignment. Intimacy with God
is my life source.
–Bill Johnson*

An elderly couple, who were quite poor and had never before won anything, one day won a five-day cruise. They prepared for the big day and took along crackers and cheese to eat on board.

When it came time for the first night dinner, the elderly couple made their way to their cabin and took out their crackers and cheese and had their dinner.

The second night, they did exactly the same, but the captain noticed that they were missing.

The third night, at dinnertime, they went to their cabin to eat their crackers and cheese. This time the captain, noticing they were missing, went to their cabin and knocked on their door. When they answered the door, he asked if they were okay, explaining that he had not seen them at any of the dinners.

Rather embarrassed, they explained that they came to their cabin to eat the crackers and cheese because they could not afford the dinners.

The captain stood there for a moment, bewildered, and then said, "But you don't understand! The dinners are included in the total prize that you won."

They missed out on what was already paid for!

We can know about something and still not partake. So much has been paid for by Jesus so that we can partake of such wonderful things.

The banquet table mentioned in Psalm 23, which is set before us in the presence of our enemies, is only valuable to you if you partake of it. You can be in a room full of the most amazing food and yet starve to death unless you eat.

It is only by revelation that you receive the kingdom and that you can walk, live, and have your being in it, like a garment that you put on.

The Father's answer to all of Earth's problems, the separation between him and his people, was a son.

> *For God so loved the world that He gave His only begotten Son, that whoever believes in Him should not perish but have everlasting life.* **John 3:16**

The answer of the Father to life's difficulties is always a son.

At this point, I want to make it clear that when I talk about a son, I do not mean the male gender. I am referring to the concept of a son or the position of a son, which includes male and female. While women get to be known as sons in the kingdom, men get to become brides!

In the Old Testament, the answer to life's difficulties was a servant, but in the fullness of time, a son was born.

And Moses indeed was faith-
ful in all His house as a servant,
for a testimony of those things
which would be spoken afterward,
but Christ as a Son over His own
house, whose house we are if we
hold fast the confidence and the
rejoicing of the hope firm to the
end. **Hebrews 3:5–6**

You are qualified as a Son of God no matter your gender!

For as many as are led by the
Spirit of God, these are sons of
God. For you did not receive the
spirit of bondage again to fear,
but you received the Spirit of
adoption by whom we cry out,
"Abba, Father." The Spirit Himself
bears witness with our spirit
that we are children of God, and
if children, then heirs—heirs of
God and joint heirs with Christ, if
indeed we suffer with Him, that
we may also be glorified together.
Romans 8:14–17

There is built into all of creation an expectation that is beyond normal expectation. It is expectation on steroids, a turbo-charged expectation! All of creation is waiting for believers to realize who they are and start behaving like sons of God.

> *For the earnest expectation of the creation eagerly waits for the revealing of the sons of God.*
> **Romans 8:19**

Since Pentecost, we have become the first people to live in two realms at once, that is, on Earth and in Heaven at the same time. We are to help bring eternity into time—into the now.

Ephesians 2:6 says, "and raised us up together, and made us sit together in the Heavenly places in Christ Jesus."

Our job is to bring Heaven to Earth, as there is far too much hell on Earth. We are to Heavenize Earth.

This is the will of God: that what happens in Heaven ought to happen on Earth.

Only sons bring Heaven to Earth, for they are the ones with access to Heaven.

The answer is always a son.

The issue is therefore about identity, knowing and understanding who you are!

The enemy continues to challenge it. He will challenge you with the thought, "Who do you think you are?" He is involved in identity fraud.

Remember from the beginning of this book, the story of Jesus coming to John the Baptist to be baptized. The Father declared from Heaven, "This is my son in whom I am well pleased."

Afterward, Jesus was led by the Holy Spirit into the wilderness and fasted for forty days.

> *While he was there, Satan came to him, and the very first thing he said to him was, "If you are the Son of God then prove it by turning these stones into bread."*
> **Matthew 4:3**

The enemy was challenging the Word of God, trying to question his position and create doubt. He was also trying to reinforce the lie that you are someone because of what you do or accomplish.

Jesus defeated that lie on that day! You no longer have to live under it.

But when the fullness of the time had come, God sent forth His Son, born of a woman, born under the law, to redeem those who were under the law, that we might receive the adoption as sons.

And because you are sons, God has sent forth the Spirit of His Son into your hearts, crying out, "Abba, Father!" Therefore you are no longer a slave but a son, and if a son, then an heir of God through Christ. **Galatians 4:4–7**

To help understand the mind-set of a son and the opposing mind-set of an orphan, ponder these points:

1. A son delights to serve and do all that he can. He understands he is building his inheritance and the family business. An orphan has performance-based relationships. He sees everything as a duty or burden. He is just working for the money.

2. A son knows he is approved by the Father and is secure in that. An orphan continually seeks out approval from others.

3. A son knows love by the law of love (gracious); an orphan knows and lives by the love of law (legalistic and judgmental).

4. A son wants to walk in the holiness of his Father in Heaven and not harm that relationship. He knows that because his Heavenly Father is holy, so is he. An orphan must be holy by his own actions and often has a list of ways to be holy. Guilt and shame increase as the orphan fails to attain the required level of holiness.

5. A son knows he is accepted and valued by the Father and is very secure in that knowledge. An orphan compares himself with others and what they have, for the purpose of proving to himself that he is not accepted or valued.

6. A son is interdependent and submissive. An orphan is independent and self-reliant because he has been trained to be so.

7. A son serves from a place of love in gratitude for the unconditional love shown to him. An orphan's motives seek personal achievement and gain with fear of failure.

8. A son takes ownership of matters affecting him whether he is at fault or not. An orphan seeks to blame other people and deflect any responsibility for the events around him.

9. A son sees defeat as an opportunity to learn, regroup, and be inspired for more. An

orphan sees defeat as justification to quit the game.

10. An orphan fears the word "no" and will do amazing things to avoid hearing it, as it communicates total rejection to him. To a son, "no" is simply the other side of "yes." "No" and "yes" live together. Unfortunately in trying to avoid "no," you also avoid "yes."

You can change your thinking by actively embracing the mind-set of a son.

Time to Possess

I often visit my parents in my home city, although not as often as I should. When I go there, I walk into their house confidently and usually put the kettle on for a cup of tea. I will then go and look at what cookies my mother has baked and see what else is in the pantry to eat. I also go and look in the jar where I know she stores candy. My adult children have been shocked at my actions. I don't know why, because they do it at our home! My mother loves the fact that her eldest son comes to her place to eat her cooking. (Actually, no one bakes cookies like Mum. Don't tell my wife!)

Now, if I entered the house of another person and did the same things without their permission, I would be a thief and a burglar and would get a free ride in a police car. Go to jail! Go directly to jail and do not pass GO! Don't collect $200 either. I do not have a legal right to do that!

However, I do have a legal right to enter my parents' house. In fact, more than that, I am a delight to my parents, in going to their home and eating their cooking. I partake of my privilege as a son of the household of my parents. I am partaking of my inheritance.

In the same way, we have a legal right to take hold of the things of Heaven and release them on Earth. We are sons of the household of God. No matter what your gender is, you have the rights of sonship. We have unfettered access to the provisions and the things of Heaven. We delight our Father in Heaven when we partake of them.

We have an inheritance that is available to us now. For many people, the inheritance that Jesus obtained for them is only available when they die. That is not how inheritances work! You receive your inheritance when someone else dies. Someone else has died! Jesus Christ died so that you can receive your inheritance from the Father.

In order to appropriate this inheritance, it is important that we understand how the Bible communicates many concepts. Many concepts are described in the midst of paradoxes.

A paradox is a statement that seems to contradict itself or even sound absurd, but in reality is expressing a truth.

We live within the kingdom of Heaven amongst many paradoxes. They are best illustrated by the word "and." I call this living with Andy.

A good illustration of this is that when Jesus was on Earth, he was one hundred percent God and one hundred percent man. One hundred percent God, because he was the Son of God and was perfect—without sin. One hundred percent man because he identified with mankind, to be the sacrifice and to demonstrate how the normal Christian life is meant to be lived. If he had been only one hundred percent God, then his statement, "We would not only do what he did but even greater works," would have been impossible.

In the same manner, we are sons (children) of God and at the same time, we are becoming sons (children). This demonstrates the concept "now and not yet." We are children of God now and yet we are becoming children as we grow and mature.

It is time to partake and enjoy the benefits of sonship and agree with what Heaven has to say about you on this Earth.

I am fascinated by being a son of God and discovering what that means.

Today:

To help you change your mind-set and embrace sonship, I encourage you to make a declaration each day or more often. Say aloud that you are a child of God, and keep doing it until you can declare it confidently amongst others. This will help you reprogram your mind to the truth.

In this chapter we discovered:

1. We can know about something and still not partake.

2. The answer of the Father to life's difficulties is always a Son, and all of creation is eagerly waiting for the sons of God to behave as sons.

3. We are sons of God and we are becoming sons. Only sons bring Heaven to Earth.

4. The difference between the mind-set of a son and that of an orphan.

5. Your inheritance is waiting for you right now to claim it.

Chapter 4

The Holy Spirit

*You must be the change you wish
to see in the world.
–Mahatma Gandhi*

On January 1, 1986, I had an encounter with the Holy Spirit in Brighton, South Australia that changed my life completely. I went from knowing about the Holy Spirit to knowing him personally. I went from a coward to a courageous being in very little time. The Word of God became alive to me and I had a huge desire to read it. I now had a new way of communicating to God, who I now knew as my Father in Heaven, by speaking in tongues. I knew for the first time I was his son.

In comparison to my previous life, I now was a radical, and not everyone liked it.

This scripture came alive to me:

> *Nevertheless I tell you the truth.*
> *It is to your advantage that I go*
> *away; for if I do not go away, the*
> *Helper will not come to you; but*
> *if I depart, I will send Him to you.*
> **John 16:7**

I remember people asking me what had happened to me, why I was different. My normal life had been turned upside down, and now I was living a new normal.

War had been declared, and a fight was on against a life that had been known as "normal."

A kingdom life is meant to be a life above the average and far above normal. We are meant to be living a transforming life rather than a conforming life; living a life that challenges the normality all around us. Transformation is a complete miraculous change just like that illustrated by the process of the caterpillar changing to the butterfly. The Holy Spirit is waiting to see that sort of change in the lives of people. He is ready to help that sort of change take place. Instead, many people prefer to keep conforming to what has always been, living normal lives, and living as they have always done.

The religious mind-set likes to take what was meant to be a lifestyle and turn it into an event. The life is taken out of the lifestyle, and all you have left is a style, an event.

So it's okay, well, more than okay to be called abnormal or radical. You have permission to pursue transformation and reject living life as you have always done. It's time, my friends, to rewrite the definition of what normal is. It's time for a "new normal."

A radical person is one who holds or follows strong convictions and is sometimes called an extremist.

As you can see, a radical is someone or who brings about fundamental change. That sounds like Heaven coming to Earth to me.

One of the names of the Holy Spirit is the Comforter. The Father called him that because one of his roles is to comfort us. That must mean that he knew we would be uncomfortable at times. Many people never give the Holy Spirit an opportunity to comfort them because they don't step out of their comfort zone.

The comfort zone is only meant to be a resting place, not a place of residence.

After Pentecost and their encounter with the Holy Spirit, the disciples were described like this:

*But when they did not find them,
they dragged Jason and some
brethren to the rulers of the city,
crying out, "These who have
turned the world upside down
have come here too."* **Acts 17:6**

The disciples were known to be so influential and radical that they turned things upside down. Maybe they were actually putting things into the right order!

When you add the total sum of a group and then divide that total by the number of those things, you will get the average. Jesus warned the church at Laodicea about being lukewarm or average in Revelation. He told them that it made him want to vomit; it made him sick. He said it was unacceptable for his people to live like that. This is what happens when you mix hot and cold, good and bad, right and wrong, comfortable and uncomfortable...you become lukewarm; you become average! When you mix black and white together, you get grey. So much of our world is living a grey existence.

One of the great men of God in the last century was Smith Wigglesworth, and he did amazing, miraculous things. Now, everyone loves Smith Wigglesworth because he is dead. When he was alive, he made everyone around him uncomfortable. Why? He had long ago decided to live a normal life as Jesus defined it and not as society defined it.

Today normal is said to be circumstances that are typical, usual, or expected. We live in a time and with society expectations that I suggest are more accurately described as subnormal, certainly as far as the scripture describes.

Things that once were called wrong are now being called right. Things that we had always believed to be harmful to life and community are now being called beneficial for society. The things that are now described as being normal are really far from normal. Fear abounds throughout society as the normal way of life. We have moved from one global crisis to another. Whether it is Y2K, a financial crisis, the warming of the planet, or the end of the world, fear is at the basis of these movements. While these are important issues, fear is never a good motivator only faith is. Fear is a very, very poor master.

The life that Jesus lived on this planet was an extraordinary life and far from normal. He challenged the religious leaders of the time, declaring that there was a new normal lifestyle to be lived. He taught the people of his time by revelation and insight about life from a kingdom of Heaven perspective. He described how life was meant to be lived out and how we are meant to live out our relationships with each other. He demonstrated the power of Heaven being released into everyday life circumstances to change them. He showed that the impossible was truly possible.

Jesus lived and modeled the normal Christian life. He displayed how we are meant to live and function within our communities. He did not live life as God. He put aside his divinity, to walk, live, and move as a human being. This truly is one of the great mysteries of life.

Life is not just about a set of rules or expectations. Life is not just about trying to please others. Life is not just about trying to gain things. Certainly life is never meant to be just endured. Life is meant to be enjoyed! Life is only found in one person, Jesus Christ. You can only truly live life when you know the source, the author and the holder of life, when you allow life itself to live in you.

The same is true about finding your way in life and finding the truth. All of those concepts are a person. Life is a person, Jesus Christ!

There is a conspiracy afoot; there is a plan in action. The enemy is out to get what you own, just like a thief. He is out to steal your destiny, your hope for the future, and your joy of living. The good news is that Jesus has far more power and has complete authority to enable you to experience life. I mean life as it was meant to be lived!

There is a call echoing around the nations. It's a call to exercise the power and authority of the kingdom of Heaven. It is time for the normality of the kingdom of Heaven to be rediscovered. It is time for the things Jesus taught to be exercised, to be experienced, to be lived.

This will take time, effort, and intentionality. This will take humility and a willingness to submit to God and lay aside agendas. People who embark on this course will be subject to ridicule from the keepers of normality and from those who prefer the comfort of the past to the excitement of the future. I understand that it is easier to go with the flow of those around you rather than swim against it. It is easier to walk in ruts already deeply worn in the roadway of life rather than to create a new pathway. However, the reward for refusing to change is a life that is described as a whimper rather than a roar, an unfulfilled life rather than a fulfilled one, and a life of regrets rather than a life of accomplishments.

There is no place to stay where you are. You are either changing or you are going backwards. Doing nothing is not an option. There exists in nature a law of deterioration, which declares that anything left alone will decay. Take an apple for instance, picked from the tree, separated from its life source and left sitting on a table. It will decay. It will deteriorate. It may even look okay on the outside for a little while until the external catches up with the internal condition. Then you have something far from the original, something that is fit for nothing!

In order to overcome an existing behavior, it is necessary to embrace a need for change. Firstly, it's time to repent; remember, that means to change the way you think, to change the information you have received and believed. Secondly, you need to adopt a new set of actions and way of living and begin to implement them.

The key to breakthrough is to always follow through. Many people have had breakthrough moments in their lives, but they have failed to fully experience the breakthrough they have so wanted. They thought the breakthrough came at that moment, not realizing that that was just the beginning. They needed to walk out the breakthrough, to continue to push through resistance and establish a new normal in their lives.

When you are working on breaking through mind-sets and attitudes, you will need to operate in the opposite way to your existing behavior. At first this can seem like acting "over-the-top" or just not "normal," but it is necessary to break the previous behavior. The breakthrough has more to do with establishing new behaviors, mind-sets, and attitudes than trying to defeat and evict the old ones.

Let me illustrate that by describing the arm wrestling contest that is often used by men to demonstrate their superior strength over each other.

They start with their hands locked together in a neutral position with their elbows on a table or bar top. Their aim is to get the arm of the other to touch the table top, to overpower the other. There can only be one winner. As long as each participant applies the same strength as the other, they will stay in a neutral position, in a "Mexican standoff." It is when one participant uses more force than the other that he will begin to make headway and finally take the winner's crown. Obviously he must use more force than the other to overpower him.

It is the same way when you are breaking through a mind-set, attitude, or spirit. You have to exert more effort than what you have been doing. Otherwise you stay in a neutral position and keep experiencing the same things over and over. Discouragement comes when you think that because you are applying some effort, things ought to change—when in fact, you are applying only enough force to just remain in a neutral position. Now, let me say here that I am not discounting the work of the Holy Spirit and am not saying it is all about your own effort. I am talking about operating by the leading and power of the Holy Spirit in an opposite spirit to what you have been doing.

Let me further illustrate the point. Let's say that you have an attitude of poverty. That means you tend to want to hold on to all you have and rarely give anything away. You are not a generous person. Proverbs describes poverty as the withholding of more than you ought. So primarily, poverty is about withholding.

Therefore, you decide that this is not the way to live, and you begin to change how you think about giving. You begin to understand that the Father is a great giver and that he is immensely generous. You are reminded that because he so loved the world, he gave his son. You see that, as this is his nature, you too ought to live a life of generosity. Great! Now you need to begin doing just that. Just being a hearer of the Word is not enough; you must begin to be a practitioner of the Word.

You now begin to act generously. However, just a little will keep you in a neutral place. You need to be over-the-top generous...outrageously generous, abnormally generous! This will seem really uncomfortable, and people will wonder what is wrong with you. You have lived one sort of life and become comfortable with it. Living outside of that comfort zone will feel very uncomfortable. That is why one of the names of the Holy Spirit is the Comforter. He is waiting to have the opportunity to comfort you. He wants to help you feel comforted among changes and experiences that feel anything but comfortable to you.

Generosity is not all about money, but it does include it. Giving a smile to someone who did nothing to deserve it, thanking the checkout person at the supermarket, writing cards to different people every day to thank them for being who they are, putting some money in another person's parking meter, doubling your church giving...the list goes on. You see, this is about attacking the issue in the opposite manner or the opposite spirit.

Jesus taught this concept when he introduced a new standard for living. He taught us that operating in the opposite spirit and action had more power in it than merely reacting to present circumstances.

> *You have heard that it was said,*
> *"An eye for an eye and a tooth for*

> *a tooth." But I tell you not to resist
> an evil person. But whoever slaps
> you on your right cheek, turn the
> other to him also. If anyone wants
> to sue you and take away your
> tunic, let him have your cloak
> also. And whoever compels you
> to go one mile, go with him two.*
> **Matthew 5:38–41**

Much has been written and taught about spiritual warfare, and much of that is insightful and helpful. However, I would like to simplistically define spiritual warfare as operating in the opposite spirit, as Jesus taught us in the above passage.

When you exercise your authority by operating in the opposite way to your desires or what your flesh demands or what is considered a normal response, you are declaring the heart and attitude of Heaven. Power to overcome is released as you operate in an opposite manner.

> *Again I say to you that if two of
> you agree on earth concerning
> anything that they ask, it will be
> done for them by My Father in
> Heaven. For where two or three*

> *are gathered together in My name, I am there in the midst of them.* **Matthew 18:19**

The power of agreement is a principle that works in our lives whether we realize it or not. It affects our relationships on a daily basis. Many people fail to understand that they are using this principle by agreeing with the wrong things. We are either agreeing with the Father and Heaven or we are agreeing with the enemy and hell. So often we think it's just an opinion and it does not really matter what we believe or declare.

> *That if you confess with your mouth the Lord Jesus and believe in your heart that God raised Him from the dead you will be saved.* **Romans 10:9**

What we agree with is very important, and what we declare is even more important. The above scripture describes a mystery. What comes first, the declaration, the confession, or the belief? It is a bit like the chicken and the egg question. Which one came first? There really is no suitable answer.

The answer is that both need to be in agreement with Heaven. The fact is that when you believe something, you speak about it, and because you are declaring it, you believe it even more.

> *So then faith comes by hearing,*
> *and hearing by the word of God.*
> **Romans 10:17**

Another process that helps us find what is normal for life is what Jesus described to the people around him when he said,

> *Ask, and it will be given to you;*
> *seek, and you will find; knock,*
> *and it will be opened to you. For*
> *everyone who asks receives, and*
> *he who seeks finds, and to him*
> *who knocks it will be opened."*
> **Matthew 7:7–8**

Here exists another mystery involving the effort of man that seems to invoke the provision of the Father, while remaining within the truth that he is sovereign. The Father wants us to participate in the discovery of things.

The words ask, seek, and knock, used in the passage above, are continuous tense words. That means there is no end to the asking or the seeking or the knocking. Many of us think that once ought to do it! Asking or seeking once, or one knock, ought to be enough. Those of us who are parents are accustomed to nagging and know what it is to be asked hundreds of times "Are we there yet!" when going on a journey. Well, it seems that the Father loves what we call nagging!

The process of asking, seeking, and knocking actually prepares us for the stewardship of the very thing we have been asking or seeking for. In other words, the process of finding what we are looking for prepares and equips us for the proper use of it.

In the book of Proverbs, the writer details this very point:

> *It is the glory of God to con-*
> *ceal a matter, but the glory of*
> *kings is to search out a matter.*
> **Proverbs 25:2**

The Father loves to hide things for us and not from us. He loves to watch us search for something he has hidden. Parents often play games with their children by hiding things for them to find. The objective is for the children to find the objects, so they are hidden in obvious places. The parents want their children to find them, so they don't put them in places where they will never be found. So it is with our Heavenly Father. He loves to conceal things for us to find and then watch us in the process of seeking.

The Father knows that if we find something prematurely, we will cause ourselves and others more harm than good. He also knows that we are responsible for the stewardship of the things that we find. He therefore creates a process that matures and develops us in the seeking, in the asking, and in the knocking.

On the December 14, 2007, divers in shallow waters off the Dominican Republic found the wreckage of a ship abandoned by Captain William Kidd in the seventeenth century.

The story goes that Captain Kidd captured the Quedagh Merchant, which was loaded with valuable satins and silks, gold, silver, and other East Indian merchandise. He left the ship to sail to New York and then on to London to clear his name of piracy charges. It seems the crew most likely sank the ship. He was subsequently found guilty of the charges and hanged. Unfortunately, such a valuable ship was lost.

It was remarkable that this ship remained undiscovered for some three hundred years. The divers discovered the ship just seventy feet (twenty-one meters) off the coast of Catalina Island and in less than ten feet (three meters) of crystal clear, pristine water. For three hundred years, people had been searching for this ship, and it was there all the time. I wonder how many times people had traveled over the ship. How many times had searchers looked in the vicinity but not found what they were looking for? The ship was amazingly intact; looters had not found it either, and that is a rare thing.

One of the search team, Charles Beeker, said, "When I first looked down and saw it, I couldn't believe everybody had missed it for three hundred years. I've been on thousands of wrecks and this is one of the first where it's been untouched by looters."

Remember, the ship was located seventy feet from the shore and in less than ten feet of crystal clear water, yet was somehow hidden from everyone.

You will only find when you seek, when you go looking for things hidden so that you can find them in the looking. It is the process of seeking that prepares you for the living out of what you find.

I am fascinated with being a radical!

Today:

To remind you of the importance of exercising a gift of the Spirit, I encourage you speak in tongues, if you have that gift, pray, and ask for new languages. If you don't speak in tongues, then ask for the ability; believe and then speak, persevering until you do!

In this chapter we discovered:

1. We are meant to be living a transforming life rather than a conforming life, living a life that challenges the normality all around us.

2. The comfort zone is only meant to be a resting place, not a place of residence.

3. There is no place to stay where you are. You are either changing or you are going backwards. Doing nothing is not an option.

4. The power of agreement is a principle that works in our lives whether we realize it or not.

5. The Father loves to hide things for us and not from us. He loves to watch us search for something he has hidden.

6. Breakthrough has more to do with establishing new behaviors, mind-sets, and attitudes than trying to evict the old ones.

Chapter 5

Earnest Expectation

There is no easy walk to freedom anywhere, and many of us will have to pass through the valley of the shadow of death again and again before we reach the mountaintop of our desires.
–Nelson Mandela

All people love change–until it affects them! Attitudes and mind-sets are like a baby's diaper–unless you change it, sooner or later it will stink.

Effective sons of God know that their Father is taking them from glory to glory, and they embrace change instead of enduring or fighting it.

For at least the last fifty years, the body of Christ has been transitioning out of the church era and into the kingdom era.

This is a change from "going to church" to "being the Church."

This is a change from attracting people to the church to be saved, ministered to, healed, and delivered to being the people of God, going to others, and seeing them set free.

The role of the people in church has changed from that of spectators to participants of the Great Commission.

The role of the pastor has changed from that of Superman to the facilitator of people's gifts and callings.

The best days of the church are still before it.

Your best days are still ahead of you—tomorrow will be better than yesterday. If you don't believe that, then you have believed a lie.

Any area of your life where you have no hope then it's under the influence of a lie. **Bill Johnson**

Hope is the earnest expectation for good, anticipation, a confident expectation.

So if you can't see your best days ahead of you then you have believed a lie.

Some people tell me that they are disillusioned by the Church or leadership or some other event.

Well, let's take a moment and examine the word disillusioned...

"Dis-" means the removal of something, and an illusion is something that was never really there. So the removal of something that was never really there seems to be a crazy reason to stay bitter all the rest of your life.

> *Now may the God of hope fill you with all joy and peace in believing, that you may abound in hope by the power of the Holy Spirit.*
> **Romans 15:13**

Now may the God of hope, that is, a God who is hope, someone who has a confident expectation and anticipation of good for you and your future, may he fill you! That is, literally cram into you, like filling something to overflowing or filling a hollow in the ground so that it is flooded.

But fill you with what? Fill you with joy and peace.

The seedbed of hope is joy and peace. Joy and peace are fruit of the Spirit. They are the result of the work of the Holy Spirit in your life; they are evidence of his activity in your life.

Galatians 5:22 says, "But the fruit of the Spirit is love, joy, peace, long suffering, kindness, goodness, faithfulness, gentleness, self-control. Against such there is no law."

Seriousness is not a fruit of the Spirit, although some think it is.

The desire of the Father is that joy and peace are so abundant in your life that they will cause you to believe, believe that you can abound in hope! This is not about self-effort; there is no try-harder Christianity here! This is something the Father wants to happen in your life more than you do. He is waiting for your green light, for you to yield yourself, for you to get over yourself.

> *For the Kingdom of God is not eating and drinking, but righteousness and peace and joy in the Holy Spirit.*
>
> *For he who serves Christ in these things is acceptable to God and approved by men.* **Romans 14:17**

While I love to feast with eating and drinking, I know the writer is not forbidding these things. He is saying that the more important things of righteousness, peace, and joy should be expressed in and through your life.

The joy of the Lord is your strength. It's where you get your ability to persevere.

> *For the joy of the Lord is your strength.* **Nehemiah 8:10**

We are made for joy. We are created in the image of God and created for joy. Therefore joy needs to have an exit place. It is so wrong to read about joy, speak about it, and yet never laugh! The scriptures tell us that laughter is like medicine to our body.

I am surprised at a church that is more concerned about excess than the lack of things, at people who are ready to criticize others because they are laughing too much in a church service. Doesn't that seem odd? Where there is an excess of joy, surely Heaven has come to Earth. Where there is a lack of joy, surely we should be concerned.

Unfortunately some Christians are not good advertisements for God. They look like they were baptized in lemon juice.

This is why in the Old Testament, he told the people this:

> *Because you did not serve the*
> *Lord your God with joy and glad-*
> *ness of heart, for the abundance*
> *of everything, "therefore you*
> *shall serve your enemies, whom*
> *the Lord will send against you,*
> *in hunger, in thirst, in nakedness,*
> *and in need of everything; and*
> *He will put a yoke of iron on your*
> *neck until He has destroyed you."*
> **Deuteronomy 28:47–48**

The Father was telling everyone that if they misrepresent to other people that serving God is anything other than joyful, then there are repercussions. He does not want to be misrepresented. We are to represent Heaven to Earth; that is, re-present, present again a life of joy and gladness no matter what the circumstances.

We live under grace, but still these truths must apply at an even higher level, because we have the joy-giver living in us.

We serve a God of abundance, and there ought to be abundance wherever he is manifesting himself.

The enemy can't take your destiny from you; he can't steal your ministry or your prophetic words, but if he can steal your joy, then you give away what you have. In that situation, he wins.

Joy is not based on circumstance; that's happiness.

A study revealed this about happiness:

Finding money in an old pair of jeans, having a picnic in the sun, getting flowers or chocolates from a loved one or a thank you card in the mail are some of the things that make people feel happy.

A person being told that he or she has lost weight, climbing into bed with freshly washed sheets and seeing an old couple hold hands also help brighten a person's day, says the study of 3,000 people conducted by Three Barrels Brandy.

Sunshine was found to be one of the major factors for happiness. Waking up to a sunny day, sitting in the sun, having a picnic in the sun, and driving with the car windows down on a sunny day all appear in the top 20, the Daily Express reported.

"We can be having a terrible day at work when a quick thank you from the boss can pick us up and make us feel great. Similarly, we could be stuck in traffic when our favorite song comes on the radio and makes us forget about the nightmare daily commute," a research spokesman said.

Most people feel at their happiest at around 6 pm Saturdays, the research revealed.

Happiness is based on circumstances, while joy exists despite the circumstances and carries us through the obstacles, challenges, and difficulties.

Remember, Jesus was able to endure the cross because of joy—joy that was set before him. Joy enabled him to walk on through the things that make you cringe just thinking about them, horrendous things. Joy is our ability to keep on going.

If you are going through hell, then don't stop.

> *...looking unto Jesus, the author and finisher of our faith, who for the Joy that was set before Him endured the cross, despising the shame, and has sat down at the right hand of the throne of God.*
> **Hebrew 12:2**

The work has been done for you.

Some years ago I was in Pakistan with a team, preparing to teach pastors on the gifts of the Spirit and to minister to them. We were in the capital Islamabad waiting to go to the meeting place. That morning I woke up and could not get out of bed. My body was wracked with pain and I could not move. The team came into my room and started to pray. I remember seeing the team leader, Roger, sitting on a small table and praying seriously in tongues. Suddenly he started to laugh so hard that his belly was bouncing up and down. Spontaneous laughter broke out amongst all the team in the room and I also started to laugh. All the pain disappeared and I was up and out of bed. Joy is indeed a destroyer of sorrow!

The Father expects us to act like him. He calls things that aren't as if they are. Laugh when you least feel like it and see how things change. Call your difficult day a joy-filled day, and see what happens.

> *God, who gives life to the dead*
> *and calls those things which do*
> *not exist as though they did;*
> **Romans 4:17**

Graeme Cooke says, "There are no good or bad days; there are only days of grace."

> *Rejoice always and again I say*
> *rejoice.* **Philippians 4:4**

This is a deliberate choice to have joy again and again, to stir up the joy and let it out.

Choosing Hope

Abraham illustrates to us what it means to choose to hope. His circumstances seemed hopeless, and yet he chose to hope.

> *Abraham who, contrary to hope, in hope believed, so that he became the father of many nations, according to what was spoken, "So shall your descendants be."* **Romans 4:18–25**

Hope is a choice!

> *Hope deferred makes the heart sick, but when the desire comes, it is a tree of life.* **Proverbs 13:12**

This scripture is referring to the decision of people to give up hope.

Abraham waited for many, many years, and circumstances only got worse. Yet despite his efforts, he still hoped that something would happen.

There are some people today who have "heart sickness" because they have stopped hoping.

Hope is the seedbed of faith. Hope is the parent of faith. Hope is not faith, and faith is not hope. Faith is the result of hope coming into actuality.

Now faith is the substance of things hoped for, the evidence of things not seen. **Hebrews 11:1**

So much has been taught about faith and love, and now hope is showing us the way.

And now abide faith, hope, love, these three; but the greatest of these is love.
1 Corinthians 13:13

Lost hope is the undertaker's best friend.

*Return to the stronghold, you prisoners of hope.
Even today I declare, that I will restore double to you.*
Zechariah 9:12

Maybe as a prisoner of hope, we are bound to expectancy; we are bound to the God of all hope

Prisoner means being yoked to, hitched to, and fastened to, to join the battle. To whom are you a prisoner?

I am fascinated with being filled with joy and peace and abounding in hope.

Today:

I encourage you to intentionally do things that will assist in increasing your joy level. Laughter is good medicine, so how about you watch a comedy, read a funny book, or look in the mirror and laugh. Make yourself laugh; just laugh.

In this chapter we discovered:

1. For at least the last fifty years, the body of Christ has been transitioning out of the church era and into the kingdom era.

2. Hope is the earnest expectation for good, anticipation, a confident expectation.

3. The desire of the Father is that joy and peace are so abundant in your life that they will cause you to believe, believe that you can abound in hope.

4. The enemy can't take your destiny from you; he can't steal your ministry or your prophetic words, but if he can steal your joy, then you give away what you have. Don't allow that to happen.

Chapter 6

Transformation

Insanity: doing the same thing over and over again and expecting different results.
–Albert Einstein

One morning I went to preach in a church an hour from my home. As I drove there, I meditated on a saying I had heard the day before. It went like this: "If you always do what you have always done, then you will always get what you have always got!"

I had no idea what that saying was going to do; my life was about to change. The thought became so overwhelming that I had to change my message and preach on it instead. Over the coming months and years, the Father would not let me preach anything else! I even begged him to let me preach something else. However, whenever I prepared something else, it always became clear that I was to preach the message about changing the way you think. I came to understand it was more about me getting it; more about my own thinking being challenged. It was almost as though I were preaching it so I would get it. I began to see that things had to change. I could not keep doing what I had been doing and expect, miraculously, different results. That was just not logical. I had no idea what was to come, how my world was going to be turned upside down.

It had been said of the disciples in Acts 17:6 that "These who have turned the world upside down have come here too." I understand that they were able to turn the world upside down because their own world had first been turned upside down by the revelations of God about his kingdom on this earth.

Since that time I have been on a mission of change for myself, embarking on a journey to discover why I behaved as I did and how to help others change. Let me emphasize that change in a person's life is only possible by the work of the Holy Spirit. However, being open to that change, positioning yourself for change, and making a decision to change will make it possible. Your natural actions can position you for supernatural change.

Jesus began his ministry with these words from Matthew 4:17: "Repent, for the Kingdom of Heaven is at hand."

Many people have an understanding of repentance as something that you do on occasion, more like an event. When someone comes to the front of a church meeting to accept Christ, or to return to him or to confess some wrong behavior, we call that repenting. That is wonderful and important, but it is the fruit of repentance.

To repent means to change the way you think. Therefore, repentance is meant to be a lifestyle and not just an event. Religion loves events. It loves to take something that is meant to be a living, effective part of your life and turn it into an event, something you visit on rare occasions because you have to.

Jesus began his ministry by telling everyone that the kingdom of Heaven was at hand, and that in order to understand and walk in it, you had to change your thinking. Your current thinking would not be able to take you into the new season. It had been able to get you this far, but couldn't take you into the new, into the kingdom ways; you had to change the way you think.

Paul seemed to understand this perfectly:

> *And do not be conformed to this world, but be transformed by the renewing of your mind, that you may prove what is that good and acceptable and perfect will of God.* **Romans 12:2**

> *Transformation in the world happens when people are healed and start investing in other people.* **Michael W. Smith**

You will either conform or be transformed. If you are not transforming, you will be conforming to the ways of this world and to your previous patterns of life. The plan of the Father is always about transformation. We live in a time called the "Information Age" where you can obtain up-to-date information from the Internet. You can keep up with friends on Facebook and find out what they are doing. You can Google and find the answer to any question. You can get updates on the latest breaking news and watch things as they happen. Never before have we had so much information so easily accessible. People have become satisfied with information rather than transformation.

Transformation is the goal—nations transformed, cities transformed, and individual lives transformed.

The Greek word used for transformed is metamorphoo, and this is where we get the word metamorphosis. Metamorphosis is the process of changing from one state to a completely different one. The best illustration of this is the process by which the caterpillar turns into a butterfly.

The caterpillar creates a cocoon, and then metamorphosis takes place. At the right time, the transformed being makes a hole in the cocoon and begins the process of extricating itself. This process actually enables the newly transformed creature to be strong enough to survive. A creature is born again. It's now a butterfly!

While I have seen many butterfly houses where people pay money to view different sorts of butterflies, I have never seen a caterpillar house! People are just not interested in looking at caterpillars and their varying shades of grey and black. But they are interested in looking at what caterpillars can become: butterflies and their amazing array of colors, shapes, and sizes.

Every caterpillar is destined to fly!

Those things that were considered to be ugly pests are turned, by the process of transformation, into things of beauty.

The Father specializes in taking the ugly things in your life, things that pester you and annoy you, and turning them into beautiful things that help you fly.

I am convinced that the kingdom of Heaven operates in a very different dimension than we have thought thus far. In order for us to understand and live in it, we have to change the way we think. Many have tried to transform the kingdom of Heaven into their own image.

The Father's plan is that we need to change because he cannot.

We must move into a place where we are agreeing with Heaven rather than trying to make Heaven agree with earthly viewpoints. Heaven will only respond to things that are going to produce eternal fruit.

At the request of the disciples, Jesus shared with them a prayer. We have called it the Lord's Prayer. Unfortunately, that is not what it is. We are in trouble if it is the prayer that our Lord Jesus prayed. John 17 could be more accurately described as the Lord's Prayer.

In that prayer, Jesus taught some perfect theology about life in the kingdom of Heaven. Firstly, Jesus teaches us about relationship. He tells us that now we have become children of God, that we have been adopted into his family. We can now refer to God as our Father in Heaven. What an incredible privilege we have been given! We are no longer the sons of disobedience; we have become the sons of the most High God. We have been transformed from beggars to princes and princesses.

The language you use about God shows how close or far away you are from him. For example, people who refer to him as "the Man upstairs," "the big fella," or "the Boss" are all most likely without any relationship with God. Conversely, those people who refer to God as "Father," "Papa," and "Daddy" usually enjoy an intimate relationship with him. These people will often tend to offend others by the use of such inappropriate words for God. The majority of his people tend to refer to him as God. The sort of relationship he wants with us is that of a perfect Father with his children, a loving, intimate, two-way relationship.

We all must understand and realize that we must maintain majesty in our relationship with God. However, only knowing God majestically does not allow you to know him intimately as a Father. Your relationship must be both majestic and intimate. Either one on its own will take you out of balance.

Living like that will enable you to understand how Jesus wants us to pray for his kingdom to come to Earth.

There are strategies in Heaven for the expansion of his kingdom on this earth; strategies just waiting for the taking.

The kingdom of Heaven must come to this earth. It must infect every area of society.

Lance Wallnau and others have described vital areas for every society. He calls them The Seven Spheres of Society. They are Spirituality and Church, Family, Education, Government and Law, Media and Communication, Arts and Entertainment, and Business and Finance. Each of these areas must be a target for the kingdom to come into, because the Father has so much to say about every area of society. Remember, the Father desires transformation, not just information.

The Church is meant to obtain these strategies and develop them in all of these areas. We are meant to be proactive in this, intentionally seeking kingdom strategies.

Salt and Light

Jesus told us, the church, that we are salt to the world. Salt adds flavor and helps preserve things from decay. Whenever the salt is withdrawn from an area of society, that area loses its kingdom of Heaven flavor and begins to decay.

Jesus also told us that we are light to the world, and light causes darkness to flee. Whenever an area of society has no or very little light, darkness dominates.

The Father can give us the ability to supernaturally increase the effectiveness of salt and light in every area. He is waiting for his people to seek those strategies.

Heaven is a storehouse of many things that Earth desperately needs, and it is our privilege, joy, and responsibility to take part in seeking them out and then bringing them to Earth.

I am fascinated with transformation.

Today:

What current thoughts do you need to change? Embrace the new thought, declare it, and think on it. Possess the new thought as your own. Use words like "I think like this now, this is how I think."

In this chapter we discovered:

1. If you always do what you have always done, then you will always get what you have always got!

2. The Father specializes in taking the ugly things in your life, things that pester you and annoy you, and turning them into beautiful things that help you fly.

3. The Father's plan is that we need to change.

4. There are strategies in Heaven for the expansion of his kingdom on this earth, strategies just waiting for the taking.

5. Heaven is a storehouse of many things that Earth desperately needs, and it is our privilege, joy, and responsibility to take part in seeking them out and then bringing them to Earth.

Chapter 7

Handling the Tough Days

When the going gets tough, the tough get going.
–Joseph P. Kennedy

As much as I would like to declare otherwise, there are days that are more challenging than others. In fact, there are days that I don't feel very confident in who I am or what I am doing. On these days, it feels like a battle just to get out of bed.

However, I have learned that it is on these days that the Father gives me divine provision to enable me to walk through the day. Some will tell you to deny the difficulties and to declare that they are no longer there. That just does not make sense. The issue is that the circumstances do exist, but we are to see them from a different perspective.

Living from the kingdom of Heaven means living from a superior realm. Learning to live from that place is what Jesus taught us to pray—on Earth as in Heaven, which is the will of the Father. Learning to live from Heaven toward Earth, we are to understand that we are not fighting for victory but enforcing what has already been won.

What we then need to discover is how to walk from this reality of grace, power, and perspective of Heaven.

A perspective is an attitude or way in which a person views a specific set of circumstances. A position a person holds on a subject or view is also their perspective.

One of my favorite accounts in the Old Testament is found in 2 Chronicles 20 and details the battle that King Jehoshaphat has come to face.

Jehoshaphat has just returned from reforming the administration of justice among his people and establishing the correct religious system. He has probably come home to rest and to enjoy the fruit of his work, to watch how things, now in order, will work throughout the kingdom.

Just then the news comes that he is not ready for. Someone tells him that the enemy is coming. (Don't you love 'the somebodies' in your life?) A great multitude is advancing toward them.

Fear comes upon the king and he sets out to seek the Lord and to declare a fast for the whole nation. He and his people begin to cry out to the Lord, reminding the Lord of all that he has previously done for them.

In the midst of this, he makes this declaration:

> *For we have no power against this great multitude that is coming against us; nor do we know what to do, but our eyes are upon You.*
> **2 Chronicles 20:12**

Jehoshaphat declares a right perspective; he says that their victory is not going to come by his might or by his strength but by the power of God.

The same thought is declared in **Zechariah 4:6**: This is the word of the Lord to Zerubbabel: "Not by might nor by power, but by My Spirit," says the Lord of hosts.

It is an important concept to grasp, that all of our brilliant ideas, effort, and determination will not amount to anything long lasting.

The Father wants us to be reminded about who sustains us and enables us.

> *....who fed you in the wilderness with manna, which your fathers did not know, that He might humble you and that He might test you, to do you good in the end— then you say in your heart, "My power and the might of my hand have gained me this wealth."*

> *And you shall remember the Lord your God, for it is He who gives you power to get wealth, that He may establish His covenant which He swore to your fathers, as it is this day.* **Deuteronomy 8:16–17**

It is an important concept that the Father is very, very keen for us to understand who is the provider and who is the receiver of that provision. That it is he who gives us the power to live and move.

He knows that we are capable of getting so much for ourselves. He also knows that we are capable of destroying ourselves. He wants to be our provider because he knows best for us.

As he waits, Jehoshaphat receives a word from the Lord, which has become a favorite for so many people to claim and quote from: Do not be afraid nor dismayed because of this great multitude, for the battle is not yours, but God's. **2 Chronicles 20:15** Remember, we, as a people of the New Covenant, always fight from a place of victory and not for victory.

Further instructions come from the Lord:

> *You will not need to fight in this battle. Position yourselves, stand still and see the salvation of the Lord, who is with you, O Judah and Jerusalem!' Do not fear or be dismayed; tomorrow go out against them, for the Lord is with you."* **2 Chronicles 20:17**

Here is the strategy that the Father gives to Jehoshaphat and to the people. They are to position themselves and then stand and watch what he is going to do. They are to take on a mind-set that the battle is already won. That God is going to do the fighting. That it is his battle.

When you position yourself in your mind for victory, you are in a different place than when you are still trying to work out how to do it. It is a shift from one mind-set to another.

When you change position in sitting because the old position was too uncomfortable, you have embraced a new place. Sometimes a physical positional shift is needed. A physical stance can demonstrate an intention. A fighting stance indicates an intention to fight or defend yourself. The raising of hands or the waving of a white flag indicates a desire to surrender.

When you embrace some new thinking because you can now see more clearly, you have changed positions. So often we value our present mind-sets, which we have fought for, so much that we are unwilling to change them.

By taking a position, a new position, Jehoshaphat understands what he is to do next. He sends out the worshippers and they defeat the enemy. Victory is theirs and they do not have to fight for it.

Remember that the concept in scripture is first in the natural and then in the spiritual. **1 Corinthians 15:46**

Whatever You Acknowledge

Whatever you acknowledge, it will direct your path.

> *Trust in the Lord with all your heart, and lean not on your own understanding; In all your ways acknowledge Him, and He shall direct your paths.*
> **Proverbs 3:5–6**

We are made to trust in something or lean on something in order to live life. We get to choose what we lean on.

You will lean on something, either God or your own understanding. If you lean on God, he will give you understanding, but it may seem irrational!

If you lean on your understanding, you will rationalize God and the supernatural out of the picture before you know it.

There is great pressure on many people to lean on their own understanding. "When I see it, I will believe it" has turned into "When I understand it, I will believe it."

The phrase "yes, but" becomes the favorite saying of those who trust in their own understanding, so you could say they have big buts.

Whatever you acknowledge, it will direct your path. It sets a guiding light; it directs your vision to the things that are in front.

To acknowledge means to recognize, to perceive, to know!

If you acknowledge lack, then that's what you will find; you go looking for it. You will see lack everywhere. All you hear is lack, and then your mind helps confirm the situation.

You won't be looking for provision or abundance; you'll only be looking for lack, so you won't find abundance. You'll create a path toward lack because you will find what you are seeking.

You must not even acknowledge those thoughts. You have to remove that word from your vocabulary.

You must live in denial—denying the lies, believing the truth, and declaring it, the truth as Heaven sees it.

God has created us with a part in our brain to help us accomplish this. It is called the reticular activating system (RAS). This part of the brain decides which bits of information get in and which are ignored. As we are literally exposed to billions of pieces of information every minute, the RAS functions as an editor to sort through all that information.

For instance, imagine you are looking for a new car, say a red Mazda 6. You take it for a test drive and are very interested in its performance. You take it back to the showroom and leave to think about the deal. While driving along the freeway, you pass several red Mazda 6 sedans. In fact, they are all over the place! They must have suddenly appeared. No, they were there all the time, but your reticular activator is now looking for them.

Whatever you look for, you will find it! Whatever you acknowledge, it will direct your path.

Many Christians are focused on excess; that is, they fear going into excess. They fear going into abundance.

I want to fear lack more than I am concerned about excess.

> *I don't listen to warnings about excess from people that are satisfied with lack!*
> **Bill Johnson**

Whatever You Magnify

David, who had been anointed king by the prophet Samuel, gathers together a mighty army. He has been fleeing from King Saul, who wants to kill him. He begins to build his army with "Everyone who was in distress, everyone who was in debt, and everyone who was discontented." (1 Samuel 22:2) These are the rejects of society, the people that nobody wants, not the best recruits for any army.

David spends time with the men, developing and training them. He teaches them how to fight and how to be a united band of mighty men. He invests in them and pours his life into their lives.

David sees such potential in them and works to develop that potential. The rest of the society sees them as rejects. He has belief in these men and believes that they can become useful to the work of the Lord. David becomes the captain of this army and starts with about four hundred men. He adds to the number, bringing it to around six hundred.

Ziklag is their home and base camp where their families live together with all their possessions. Having been rejected by Saul and his people, David and his mighty men go down to Aphek to join with the Philistines to fight against

Israel. However, they too reject David and his men from fighting with them. It is a bad day when even your enemy rejects you.

So with rejection all about them, David and his men return to Ziklag. As they are nearing the city, they see smoke rising—not just the smoke from the cooking fires, but thick smoke, large volumes of smoke. Their hearts are racing as they near the city. This is not right, something has gone wrong.

The Amalekites, their enemies, came to the camp while they were gone and took their women, children and all their possessions. They burned the camp to the ground and robbed them of all their valuables.

When they arrive at the camp, David and his men see the devastation and find that their loved ones are missing. Understandably, they are distraught. All the men are crying out in desperation, and they cry until they have no more energy to cry. Their distress is beyond imagination. They have lost everything! David is in the same place, and he is grieved beyond description. He, too, has experienced the loss of his own family. He grieves also for the loss of the families of his men.

Out of their distress, the men start talking about stoning David. So often, when difficulties arise, people will look to take their distress out on their leaders; because they cannot handle the pain themselves, they project the blame onto those who are leading them. Unfortunately, this is all too common. People fail to take responsibility for their own actions and instead blame others for their experiences. Human nature seems to love to play the blame game. Ever since Adam told God that the woman he had given him was the problem, mankind has looked for someone to blame. You will notice that David does not respond to this, nor does he try and blame anyone else.

What he does is go and a find a place by himself and begins to strengthen himself in the Lord. David does not go to God complaining or asking why this has happened. He does not blame God. He goes to worship the Lord, to magnify him in the midst of these distressing and painful circumstances.

I am sure he would begin by reminding himself who God is and declaring how great a God he serves. He would declare that the Father is good and that his mercies endure forever. He knows that the Father inhabits the praises of his people. He creates a place for God to inhabit in the midst of terrible circumstances, circumstances that are certainly not ideal, circumstances that are very, very painful. Heaven is never moved by need, but it is moved by a heart positioned to praise the Father.

David positions himself to hear from the Lord, taking himself out of the very real grief that he is feeling. He puts himself in a place to hear what the Lord is saying about the circumstances and the solution. He wants the perspective of Heaven about his earthly situation, and he gets it.

He asks of the Lord, "Shall I pursue this troop? Shall I overtake them?" In other words, can we go get our wives, our children, and our possessions back? The Lord says to David, Pursue, for you shall surely overtake them and without fail recover all. **1 Samuel 30:8**

Then, after hearing the Word of the Lord, he goes back to the men, the grieving, hurting, we-are-going-to-stone-you men, and tells them they are going to go and get everything back. Miraculously they come out of their grief, forget their desire to stone David, and are energized to go and get back what had been stolen. What has happened?

They have heard from David the Word of the Lord. It is so empowering and strengthening to hear the Word of the Lord. That is why it is so important to position yourself to hear from Heaven and why there is such a fight to keep you from hearing.

So often, we are overwhelmed by the worry of circumstances, by the anxiety that abounds, by the grief of situations and by the very difficult nature of life. All these experiences are very real, and yet they can trap us into a place where we cannot see correctly. Our perspective becomes distorted and we cannot see the solution; the problem just keeps getting bigger.

David so understood this principle that his lifestyle had become one of obtaining and living in right perspective.

Psalm 34 is a great example of the lifestyle that David lived. In particular, verse 3 declares, Oh, magnify the Lord with me, and let us exalt His name together.

We are made to magnify, and the Father placed this ability within our core being. We get to choose what or whom we will magnify.

To magnify something is to make it bigger, or actually to make it appear bigger. For instance, if you were to take a magnifying glass and place it over the words in this book, they would appear bigger than they actually are.

Now, we can't make God any bigger than what he is already, but, we can make him bigger in our mind and within our own world. When we do that, we are worshipping him!

When we focus on a problem and begin to worry about it, we are magnifying it, making it bigger in our mind. When we rehearse the words spoken or replay the movie of the situations we have been faced with, we magnify them. When we go over and over and over the problem, we magnify it. When we magnify something like that, we lose perspective. We become so immersed in the problem and the situation that we are unable to find a way out. We lose the ability to see the solution. When we do that, we are worshipping the problem. We have made a new idol to worship.

The battle is always about the perspective or the position that we obtain. We are designed to be so Heavenly minded that we are of earthly good.

We are meant to look from Heaven toward Earth and the things on Earth. So many Christians are earthbound people trying to touch Heaven in some way.

Religion has developed so many practices and ways to try and touch Heaven, to somehow reach God...more like the actions of a beggar than a son, or like a widow instead of a bride.

Well, I have news for you. You don't have to wait to die to get to Heaven; you can be there today and still be alive here on Earth.

When you came to Christ and you became a temple of the Holy Spirit, you were then seated in Heavenly places; (He)raised us up together, and made us sit together in the Heavenly places in Christ Jesus. **Ephesians 2:6**

We are now positioned on Earth and also in Heaven with Christ. We are the great declarers of the will of God. Remember, Jesus taught us to pray that the will of the Father was "on earth as it is in Heaven." **Matt 6:10**

I am fascinated with the power of Heaven to handle even the tough days and to release Heaven to Earth.

Today:

To help you change your way of thinking, I encourage you to develop a practice of asking this question: how am I magnifying Father in this situation or circumstance?

Are there words I am declaring that I need to change? Look for new words to replace the old words.

A good declaration is "I live from Heaven to Earth. I see things on Earth from Heaven's perspective."

In this chapter we discovered:

1. Living from the kingdom of Heaven means living from a superior realm, a realm that is an overcoming realm. Learning to live from that place is what Jesus taught us to pray...we are on Earth as in Heaven, which is the will of the Father.

2. We, as a people of the New Covenant, always fight from a place of victory and not for victory.

3. Whatever you acknowledge, it will direct your path.

4. We are made to trust in something or lean on something in order to live life. We get to choose what we lean on.

5. We are made to magnify, and the Father placed this ability within our core being. We get to choose what or whom we will magnify.

6. We are meant to look from Heaven toward Earth and the things on Earth.

Chapter 8

The Keys

*There is no passion to be found
playing small—in settling for a life
that is less than the one you are
capable of living.
–Nelson Mandela*

Jesus told Peter that he gave him the keys
of the kingdom of Heaven.

*And I will give you the keys of the
Kingdom of Heaven, and whatever
you bind on earth will be bound in
Heaven, and whatever you loose*

on earth will be loosed in Heaven."
Matthew 16:19

Keys unlock and enable entry into places you have previously not been able to access. I believe that there are so many dimensions for us to experience. There is no end to God.

The following are some of those keys that will help you to see Heaven on Earth.

Authority Is at Issue Here

Jesus said, "All authority is mine." That is 100 percent of authority, not 75 percent or 98 percent of authority. All means all. As Jesus has all authority, so it must follow that Satan has no authority. None at all, zip, zero, no authority whatsoever. However, we know Satan does seem to have some authority. So how did he get it?

Satan gets his authority from people. He tricks us, just like he did with Adam and Eve, so that we release authority to him by coming under his rule. He uses intimidation, our sin and disobedience, fear, and our agreement with his ideas.

One of the ways Satan tricks people into agreement with him involves their sense of significance. So many people today still believe that their significance is determined by what they do. We determine the importance of a person's life by the occupation they hold. Doctors, lawyers, CEOs, and many similar occupations are considered to be of more importance and value than those in other fields.

Many workers are called professionals, and those that work with their hands are called blue-collar workers. Salaries, indeed, seem to reflect this same message. Now, I know there are many things to take into consideration, and I am not saying that it is wrong to pay people for more responsibility or because they have completed many years of education and training. What I am saying is that it is wrong to determine the value of your life by the work you do.

Often the conversation among men is directed toward finding out what occupation the other is engaged in. For pastors, the question is "How many people do you have in your church?" This is another form of ranking to determine importance.

Now, if your value is determined by the work you do, what happens when you can no longer do that work or even work at all? Your value has declined substantially.

However, there is no need for this happen. People who know Jesus Christ as their own personal Lord and Savior, who have come into relationship with him and have the Holy Spirit residing in their lives, can walk in freedom from this lie. You can know in a deeper way that you are significant to the Father by being his child.

Being always comes before doing. We are human beings, not human doings. Anything out of order does not usually work, so coming into proper order causes things to work.

Jesus said that it was to our advantage that he went to be with the Father. If he had not, then the Holy Spirit would not have been able to come and take up residence in the lives of believers, children of the Father in Heaven.

When this occurs, the Holy Spirit declares to whom we belong.

> *The Spirit Himself bears witness with our spirit that we are children of God, and if children, then heirs— heirs of God and joint heirs with Christ, if indeed we suffer with Him, that we may also be glorified together.* **Romans 8:16–17**

What is needed is for us to come to an understanding that we are secure in our relationship with Jesus, that he will never leave us or forget about us. Our relationship with him is not dependent on our performance.

Agreement Is a Key

Again I say to you that if two of you agree on earth concerning anything that they ask, it will be done for them by My Father in Heaven. **Matthew 18:19**

In this verse, Jesus details an incredibly important concept, a principle of Heaven; that is, the power of agreement. Power is released when there is agreement. You can see the opposite happen too. Where there is disagreement, the removal of agreement, you can see how much disarray comes. You can feel the atmosphere around people who are in disagreement.

When you agree with the Father, then you see power for those things from Heaven to happen. When you agree with Satan, you see the power for those things from hell to happen. You get to choose with whom you will partner.

Of course there really is no choice, but you still get to choose.

That is why it is so vital for you to allow the Holy Spirit to change the way you think and to stop agreeing with the enemy about who you are. Words like, "I could never do that," "I'm not good enough for God to love me," "I am not worthy to be God's child," or "I am just a sinner," are words that agree with the enemy and empower him. Changing your speech will help you begin to understand who you are.

You need to begin to declare that you are "a child of God," "someone special," "I can do all things, because Jesus strengthens me."

Lucifer had a lust for position and power. He wanted to be like God.

We understand that God is love. He is the source of love and expects us to walk in love.

It is important to understand the basis of lust and then compare it with love.

Put simply, lust takes! All that it does is for the benefit of the taker at the expense of others. On the other hand, love gives, and all that it does is for the benefit of others at the expense of the giver.

So you can see that motive is very important, and the question we need to ask is "For whom am I doing this?"

Jesus displayed to us what life can be like. He showed us how to live a life completely surrendered to the Father and how to walk in Heaven's power on this earth.

Jesus was absolutely secure in the Father's love and acceptance. He knew that he did not have to earn the Father's love or his acceptance. That is why he could sleep in a boat in the middle of a horrendous storm! He knew who he was, and in his life there was no storm.

Insecurity is simply being secure in the wrong things, putting your security into things that won't last. Security is putting your trust in someone who is secure, someone who is always the same, someone who is faithful and trustworthy, someone just like Jesus Christ.

Follow-Through Is a Key

Everyone wants breakthrough and the release from some sort of mind-set, behavior, or attitude. Most people, however, don't usually pay the price for the breakthrough. We live in a society where "easy come, easy go" is so often experienced.

It is a simple but profound truth that you can have your breakthrough, if you will follow through with what Heaven has told you.

I have people tell me that the prophetic word they received ten years prior has not yet happened. When I read it, I see they were meant to partner with the Father and do certain things... that is, follow through.

I give people advice all the time. Many of them say things like, "You told me to do such and such years ago." I ask, "Did you do it?" Often they look rather embarrassed and tell me that they have not.

You cannot expect different results if you still do the things that got you into the situation in the first place. You need to change your ways!

The key to breakthrough is to always follow through.

Praise Is a Key

The scriptures tell us that God inhabits the praises of his people. That means that praising God attracts Heaven to Earth, brings Heaven into your earthly situation, and attracts angels.

Grumbling and complaining, according to Jude, is the praise of hell and attracts the enemy.

If you want the involvement of Heaven in your life or situation, then praise and thanksgiving will attract Heaven to your situation.

Praise is a key that will turn the lock and release the provision of Heaven on Earth.

I am fascinated with the keys of the kingdom of Heaven and with using them on Earth to unlock things.

Today:

Find your prophetic words, dust them off, and look at all of them. Find five key words, that is, words that are mentioned often. Then construct an "I Am" statement and use that to declare who you are.

Or

Go on a fast from all critical words, all grumbling, and all complaining for at least seven days.

In this chapter we discovered:

1. What is needed is for us to come to an understanding that we are secure in our relationship with Jesus, that he will never leave us or forget about us. Our relationship with him is not dependent on our performance.

2. When you agree with the Father, then you see power for those things from Heaven to happen.

3. Jesus displayed to us what life can be like. He showed us how to live a life completely surrendered to the Father and how to walk in Heaven's power on this Earth.

4. If you want the involvement of Heaven in your life or situation, then praise and thanksgiving will attract Heaven to your situation.

Chapter 9

Andrew's Experience: Heaven Comes to Earth

What mixed emotions I am feeling right now. I am so tired and hungry but, at the same time, so excited and feeling so great about all the wonderful things that have been happening all around us. I saw Jesus cause so many amazing things to happen. A young boy so terrorized by some evils spirits got totally set free, a twelve-year-old girl was raised from the dead, and an old woman was healed of a condition she had had for twelve years. We were full of excitement and amazement at how these people's lives had been transformed. I am still thinking about that twelve-year-old girl who lost her life, her destiny and dreams gone. Then Jesus raises her from the dead; she gets to live again. Her family has her back again.

Jesus also sent us to go from house to house. As we did so and we prayed, the crippled were healed, the lame walked again, and the blind got to see. Fathers who had not seen their children saw them for the first time. Demons were fleeing as we approached people, and the tormented were set free. It was breathtaking, and we were so excited. Words just cannot describe how wonderful it feels to see people's lives transformed and their needs totally met.

Then when we got back we heard of the latest thing that Herod did.

We heard that John, the one who baptized Jesus, has been executed by Herod. Suddenly, our emotions are plummeting. Such excitement we were feeling, and now such grief. We have such mixed emotions!

Jesus suggests that we go and rest away from everybody. That's music to my ears; I am starting to feel so tired.

We get in a boat and start to go to a place over the lake to rest, eat, and be together, away from the demands of all the people. It's going to be so nice and refreshing; I can feel it now.

Wait, why are all those people running around the edge of the sea to where we are going? There must be thousands of them. Well, I am sure we can convince Jesus to send them home.

But, before we can say anything to Jesus, he is teaching them and telling them about the kingdom. His teaching is inspiring and captivating them, and they want more. I am hearing really great ideas and getting some good thoughts, but I am so tired and hungry.

The sun is threatening to leave us, and darkness is approaching. It's getting late. I go to Jesus and interrupt his teaching, in an appropriate place, of course. "Jesus, it's getting late," I say. I think Judas says, "Send them away, so they can go and buy food for themselves." I reckon he is thinking about how much all this is going to cost us if Jesus keeps teaching.

Jesus surprises us with his answer. He says, "You give them something to eat." That's crazy, where can we find enough food for these people? There are about five thousand men here, let alone the women and the children. "Where would we find the money to finance that?" Judas asks.

"You feed them," says Jesus.

I look at Peter and he looks to me and then the others, and you can see the looks of amazement and worry on their faces.

Then Jesus says to us, "How many loaves do you have? Go and see."

I haven't seen any food anywhere, let alone bread. I suppose maybe someone had some hidden. Then as I am walking along, I see this little boy with something in his hands. I go over to him and ask him what he has. He shows me five small barley loaves and two small fish. It's obviously his food, and I am about to move on. But, Jesus did ask what loaves we had. So I ask the boy if we can take this to Jesus, and he says, "Okay."

As I am walking back to Jesus, I am thinking, how will this feed the crowds? Maybe this will feed Jesus, but it's not going to feed everyone else.

I take it to Jesus and he smiles at me, a smile that says, "Well done, Andrew, you have done well." I am proud and so happy on the inside, but still hungry.

Then Jesus asks us to make everyone sit down in groups of tens and hundreds. As we do so, the people seem expectant, as if they are anticipating something.

Then I watch as Jesus takes the barley loaves in both hands and raises them toward Heaven and gives thanks for them.

He then breaks them into small portions and gives some to each of us to distribute. I look at the bread and the fish and then to the crowds, and back at the bread and the fish. I think to myself, "This is not going to take long."

So I start to give some to the first person, and as I give it, I have more in my hands, more than I started with. The one I gave it to passes some to his children, and then he has more than when he started.

Suddenly the noise level explodes as people start praising God, and eating, and praising God some more.

I can hardly stand up; this is so overwhelming, so amazing and incredible. I go and give some to the little boy who gave it in the first place. I place it in his hands, and suddenly it is a big pile of food. He runs back to his family yelling and screaming. I watch as he arrives at his family, and then they start running around and yelling excitedly.

I take a small bite of the bread, and it is so fresh; in fact, I have never tasted bread like it.

It doesn't seem long before everyone has eaten all they could. We collect all the leftovers. There are twelve large baskets filled to overflowing with leftover food.

Then all I know is that Jesus had us get into a boat to finally go to rest and relax, away from everyone and the demands.

As I am lying back in the boat with the sound of the water gently lapping against it, I start to think about the day. I have just seen such an unexpected day of amazing things; miracles, repeating themselves thousands of times. Small pieces of food becoming banquets that fed whole groups of people. People everywhere were saying how good the food tasted and that they had never tasted things like that before. They tasted Heaven on Earth.

This was a day of all days, something I will remember forever, I am sure.

Today, I have seen a piece of Heaven distributed to thousands of people. The look on the faces of those hungry people will be in my mind forever. I don't think anything is impossible now, after seeing this happen.

I am just resting my eyes and enjoying the boat ride and the rest for my body.

Then all of a sudden, this storm starts, and the waves are so big and the wind so fierce—no more rest for me.

All memory of recent events seems to drain out of my mind as we try and stay in the boat and stay alive. You can feel the fear level rising in the boat.

****

Andrew and the disciples had just experienced Heaven on Earth so many times and in so many ways. But when the circumstances were adverse, and overwhelming, they seemed to quickly forget the recent victories.

Jesus rebuked them for failing to remember the miracles and to therefore operate in faith. They failed to interpret their present circumstances through the lens of Heaven and its miracle-working power.

Andrew had experienced such an amazing encounter with Heaven attacking Earth. These accounts are recorded so that we can learn not only from their victories but also their failures.

You too have seen and heard of amazing testimonies of the miracle-working power of God. Don't let the pressures of life, everyday occurrences, and adverse circumstances rob you of experiencing the fascination of Heaven in your part of Earth.

My own experiences and revelations from over twenty years have been the source of the material for this book. Some of those revelations have also been contributed to by the teaching of others. They are not just theories but practical steps that, if you take them intentionally, will allow you to change your life and the lives of other people.

I am fascinated with Heaven on Earth.

The surest way for good to prevail on Earth is for people to do something good. **Mark Crawford**

Fascinated By Heaven On Earth

I am fascinated with the truth that God is my Father in Heaven.

I am fascinated that we are made in his image.

I am fascinated in being a Son of God and discovering what that means.

I am fascinated with being a radical.

I am fascinated with being filled with joy and peace and abounding in hope.

I am fascinated with transformation.

I am fascinated with the power of Heaven to handle even the tough days and to release Heaven to Earth.

I am fascinated with the keys of the kingdom of Heaven and using them on Earth to unlock things.

I am fascinated with Heaven on Earth.

Made in the USA
Thornton, CO
06/10/24 08:36:18

ed17281e-91da-401b-bbdc-19dd828a6d3fR01